In the Name of

رحیم

MUSLIM DAILY PRAYERS

EDITED BY

ABDUL HAMID BIN-ASAD

Produced by
NO-I Publications
Chicago, Illinois

بسم الله الرحمن الرحيم

In the Name of Allah, The Beneficent, The Merciful

MUSLIM DAILY PRAYERS

Introduction by
Minister Louis Farrakhan

Commentary by: Abu A'la Maududi, Abdul Hamid Siddiqui, and Abdul Hamid Bin-Asad

1st Edition

Copyright © 1998
All rights reserved
Library of Congress Catalog Card Number pending
Produced and published by Specialty Promotions Book Company Inc.,
Chicago, IL 60649
E-mail: AS2.specialtybooks@gmail.com

Cover Design by John Glenn Omar

بسم الله الرحمن الرحيم

With the Name Allah,
The Merciful Benefactor, The Merciful Redeemer

Dedication

This book is dedicated to the many Muslims who have shared their knowledge to teach others of the fundamentals that are so necessary for the Islamic life.

بِسْــــمِ اللهِ الرَّحْمـنِ الرَّحِيمِ

With the Name Allah,
The Merciful Benefactor, The Merciful Redeemer

Contents

Contents (Continued)

بِسْمِ اللهِ الرَّحْمٰنِ الرَّحِيمِ

With the Name Allah,
The Merciful Benefactor, The Merciful Redeemer

A Textual Note

The Arabic writing ﷺ when translated to English, is the prayer said for Prophet Muhammad ﷺ. The Arabic pronunciation when transliterated into English is pronounced, "Salla Allah alayhi was sallam" and the English form is said as "Peace be upon him," and is to be mentioned in English or Arabic when the name of Prophet Muhammad ﷺ is mentioned or seen in written form.

بِسْــــمِ اللهِ الرَّحْمَنِ الرَّحِيمِ

With the Name Allah,
The Merciful Benefactor, The Merciful Redeemer

Acknowledgements

We are thankful to Allah for blessing us with the following believers who so graciously offered their time, money and service to get this book into publication. Abdul Hameed Bin-Asad, editor–for organizing the material and the books design, Sarah Hafeezah Bin-Asad for her assistance in proof-reading and editing, John Glenn Omar for the design of the cover and the illustrations, and his daughter, Kilima Njaro Afi Glenn Omar for the computer output and color separations of the book's cover, Misbahu Rufai for his editing and correcting and proof-reading the material, as well as checking the Arabic text and transliteration; Dr Mustafa Yousuf for typesetting the Arabic, checking the English and Arabic grammar to make sure that it was correct; Abdur Rahman ibn-Sultan Muhammad for recording the Arabic instruction tape that accompany the book; Jabir Herbert Muhammad for his support and longtime help in seeing that this book become a reality by initiating this work many years ago; Donathan Waliyuddin and Askia H. Bashir for their financial support and encouragement, Akbar Muhammad who made certain that Minister Louis Farrakhan was kept abreast of the progress of the book, and Maria Farrakhan Muhammad and her husband, Alif Muhammad who expeditiously saw that the material was approved by Minister Louis Farrakhan for publication.

May Allah bless all of those who helped to make this publication possible.

بسم الله الرحمن الرحيم

With the Name Allah,
The Merciful Benefactor, The Merciful Redeemer

Preface

This book is not designed to teach all of the essentials one needs to know about prayer in the Islamic Faith– such information on the subject can be found in many books on prayer published by many Islamic organizations and writers.

In an effort to speed up the learning process, several elements have been combined to make this possible. Not only does this book provide the reader with the English, Arabic and Arabic transliteration, but it also provides a tape of instructions on the correct pronunciation of the Arabic for the "Adhan (Call to Prayer) and Iqamah" and for each step of the Prayer service. Also included are additional supplications one can offer after performing the prayer service.

The size of the book is designed so that the reader can carry it during the learning process. Thus a quick review of the text can be made when one wants to refresh one's memory or study the text.

The book also has a glossary for those who want to get information on a particular Arabic word. An index has been included in order that the reader can have a quick reference source for locating a word or subject in the text.

The tape is designed with the text so that the reader can follow the text and transliteration while studying the prayer in order to learn the correct pronunciation of the Arabic.

Each step of the prayer is shown with the proper prayer position and explanation of how it is to be performed as well as what is to be recited while in that position.

Because this set of instructions are for the purpose of expediting the learning process for saying the prayers in Arabic, one should consult a more knowledgeable Muslim such as an Imam or scholar for further information about the Muslim prayers. Such books as the Ahadith of Sahih Muslim or Sahih Al-Bukhari is an invaluable resource for more information on the subject. There are also innumerable books on prayer by many scholars that should be very useful.

This subject of prayer is very important for Muslims and one should diligently seek as much information as possible pertaining to it.

بسم الله الرحمن الرحيم

With the Name Allah,
The Merciful Benefactor, The Merciful Redeemer

Al-Fatiha

(The Opening)

1. In the Name of Allah, The Beneficent,
    The Merciful.

2. All Praise is due to Allah,
    the Lord of the worlds;

3. The Beneficent, The Merciful;

4. Master of the Day of Requital.

5. Thee do we serve,
    and Thee do we beseech for help.

6. Guide us on the Right Path—

7. the Path of those upon whom
    Thou hast bestowed favors,
    not of those upon whom Thy wrath is brought down,
    nor of those who go astray.

بسم الله الرحمن الرحيم

With the Name Allah,
The Merciful Benefactor, The Merciful Redeemer

Introduction

We thank Allah, the Lord of Power, for guiding us safely through the old year, and granting us entrance into a new year. Those of us who came through the year 1998, certainly are grateful to Allah. But during the past year we may have had at least one great trial or more with some ups, and some downs. We may have learned of some bad news about sickness or death in our family. But Allah says in the Qur'an, that whenever a misfortune befalls the believer, the believer says, Allah is my Patron, and to Him is my eventual return.[1]

Whenever you have someone that is a patron of yours, that is a person that is friendly towards you. That is a person who supports you and is with you. When Allah says that He is the Patron of the believer, this means that the believer has in Allah the best Friend, the best Protector, the best Provider, and the Most Merciful of those who have mercy. He is the Most Forgiving, the Oft-Returning to forgiveness and mercy. The believer has in Allah, the Giver of life, the Sustainer of life, and the regulator of the affairs of His creatures. When a believer says that Allah is his Patron, this does not mean that everyday will be a day that will bring joy or gladness to the heart of the believer.

We may be tried severely in one way or another: in our families, in our national life or in the international life of the Muslims, yet in spite of that, we say, "Allah is our Patron, and to Him is our eventual return." What does this do for the believer? It gives us the proper attitude to face all of the ups and downs of life. Some of us think that when we believe in Allah, and say that we submit our will to do His Will, that no hardship should come into our

---

[1]Qur'an 2:156

xv

lives. That is the wrong way to think! Allah says, "Surely, I'm going to try you with something of fear, of hunger, of loss of property, and of lives and fruit, but give good news to those who are patient [and steadfast under trial]."[2]

Knowing that we have the best of Friend in Allah, no matter what [may] come our way, let us keep the attitude: "My Friend has brought this thing to my life, and I know that my Friend will see me through." Whenever Allah says that He straightens the means of subsistence for whom He pleases, and He amplifies it for whom He pleases,[3] surely that is a trial for you. But some of us think that when our means of subsistence is amplified, that it is not a trial. That is an even greater trial than the trial of the scarceness of your goods.

What will be your attitude should Allah cut your means of subsistence? Will you still give in charity or will you become niggardly and hold on to the little that you have, thinking that you will lose that too." You may not realize it, but you've already lost it, because Allah says, "Spend out of that which We have given you."[4] He didn't say how much. "But whatever you get, a portion of that belongs to Allah." Should there be a great trial for us, this coming year, we should remember that Allah is our Patron. "And no matter what the misfortune, my best Friend has allowed it, has permitted it in my life. And if my best Friend permitted this pain, this hurt, this problem, this poverty in my life, then my best Friend can take me out of it when He pleases. I just want to be in submission to His Will."

When Allah raised Prophet Muhammad, peace be upon him, He gave him a call and the Prophet responded. His heart was already being shaped for the Call. He had a tender heart. He had a heart of compassion for the suffering. He longed to see the relief of suffering, poverty, want, and oppression, because he desired what is best in life. He was a just human being even before the Call. He was a man that settled arguments with justice, thus he was known as "El-Amin" the Faithful, the Noble.

---

[2]Qur'an 1:155
[3]Qur'an 13:26
[4]Qur'an 2:3

When he received the "Call," from Allah, it was not just "a call" but "The Call." The angel Gabriel (Jibril) said to him, "Iqraa, Read [or Proclaim]." And he replied, "But I can't read." Gabriel then said, "Read in the name of your Lord Who creates man from a clot, and taught man by the pen what man knew not."[5]

And as he received that Call, he began to understand that Allah was commiting him to a mission. The very purpose that the Prophet came into existence, was to hear a call, and to respond to that call, which was to call humanity to the Path of God. Therefore, we cannot say that we follow the Sunnah (Practices) of the Prophet, peace be upon him, if we are not involved in the purpose for his existence in the world.[6]

Prophet Muhammad, peace be upon him, was to warn, to admonish and bring about the destruction of polytheism, and to make human beings worshippers of the One God alone–setting up no rival or partner with the One God, the Creator of the heavens and the earth. His assignment was to destroy tribalism, and to bring his immediate family into unity with one another by breaking up tribal customs, tribal traditions and establishing the Qur'an and the culture of the Qur'an as the way that all of the tribes should accept. Their acceptance of God's Message would lift them above their tribal customs and traditions and bring them into the culture and the Way of God as found in the Qur'an. But that was not all of his job, mission or duty.

Eighty days before he passed from among us, he left his faithful companions with an assignment that they were to "proclaim the Pilgrimage, proclaim the Hajj." Hajj to every Muslim is one of the most beautiful experiences of a Muslims life. I hope and pray that at the turn of the century, as we enter the new millennium, Allah will bless us with the thought in mind to visit the holiest spot on earth–the Holy City of Mecca, and to perform Hajj.

---

[5]Qur'an 96:1-5, see Sahih Muslim, Vol. I, pp. 96-97, 98, no. 301

[6]Imam Abdullah Yusuf Ali in his commentary to the Qur'an 96:1-5, states: "This proclaiming or reading implies not only the duty of blazoning forth God's Message, but also the duty of promulgation and wide dissemination of the Truth by all who read and understand it." Allah also says: "Surely We have sent you as a witness and as a bearer of good news, and as a warner, that you may believe in Allah and His Messenger, and may aid him and revere him..." Qur'an 48:8-9

Look at Muslims, and their attending the Jumu'ah prayers. The scholars say as-Salatul Jumu'ah, because it is congregational. We don't just wash our feet and hands as we do in ablution in preparation for the five daily prayers when we perform ablution by ourselves or with other members of our family. But when we are going to be with the extended family, we should take a complete bath (ghusl) in order not to be offensive. We should use some kind of...something that we put on our self that will not allow us to be offensive in the congregation as we come together to say our prayers. And we should look in our closet to find the best thing that we can, and put it on for the Jumu'ah congregational prayer.

In a society where we are on our jobs or where we work, we forsake the job to come to Salatul Jumu'ah. When we come to Salatul Jumu'ah, we have on different clothing, shoes, but for Hajj we take off everything that would separate us from each other because the world is filled with class consciousness.

The Prophet, peace be upon him, did not want any class among the Muslims except one class, the class of believers. Therefore, in proclaiming the Hajj, he gave us certain rituals to follow. We take off our regular clothing, and put on a seamless garment. We take off all of our jewelry or anything that would separate us and say to some unlearned person that this one is better or knows more, or that this one is a scholar, a king, or a prime minister.

When we come before Allah, we come before Him only as a servant. So when Prophet Muhammad, peace be upon him, proclaimed the Hajj," this meant the sacrifice of life at a certain point, the sacrifice of a camel, sheep, lamb or goat. Life had to be sacrificed.

The job of the Prophet is not over, because as our world of Islam has fallen, it has become divided into sects and parties, each one vying with the other due to envy and many other reasons. Our world of Islam has exalted politicians who pay homage to the powers that govern the world, rather than to the Power that governs all the worlds–Rabbil-'alamin, God Himself.

The whole world of Islam has been poisoned with racism, nationalism, sexism, and materialism. It is now a world that makes color, nationality, ethnic origin, your physical appearance some badge of honor, or your degree of knowledge or lack of it a badge of honor or dishonor, this world has to be called back to the Path of God.

We have to revitalize the whole world of Islam, and what better place than America to start the revival of Islam in this western horizon that didn't want Islam anywhere in America. America is a place that made certain that every Muslim among the slaves would be killed so that no slave would ever hear, Ash-hadu anla elaaha Ill-Allah (I bear witness that there is no god but Allah) and that we would never be able to pray in the manner that our foreparents prayed in Africa when they were Muslims.

The Qur'an was a hidden book that was in secret book departments in libraries. When I would go to the library to study the Qur'an, I had to say that I was a Muslim in order to get access to it. This is true. To get a copy of it, you had to get it from the rare book section. The Qur'an wasn't the common property of the people, because this book is the criteria that determines what is right, what is wrong, what is truth, and what is falsehood. The Qur'an is the final revelation to come to the world before the Judgment of the world. In fact, this Book is preparation for the life of the Hereafter.

America is a country that was founded on white supremacy. Even though every nation, every tongue, and every kindred lives in America, they can't get along. But in Islam, this is not the case. When we make Hajj, we see people of every race, of every color, of every nation, making their tawaf around the Kaaba, running between the hills of al-Safa and al-Marwa and stoning Shaitan (Devil) in a ritual. But now we have to stone Shaitan in reality by stoning the things in us that keep us from worshipping the pure worship of the One God.

Allah says to Prophet Muhammad, peace be upon him. "Call to the Way of your Lord with goodly exaltation and in the best manner."[7] Allah is telling the Prophet, "I called you, and you answered My Call, now call them. But call them in the best manner. Call them in a good voice, and call them with justice." It means that the invitation to Islam must be extended by everyone who

---

[7]Qur'an 16:125

claim to be a Muslim. If you pass by people in their wretched condition, and never invite them to what you were invited to; that has cleansed and begun the process of purifying your life, then you have failed the Prophet. And his mission has died with you.

When you come to the masjid and say your prayers, you have benefitted, but who are you benefiting? Some of you may disagree with what I am about to say, but the Honorable Elijah Muhammad, when we dedicated the Mosque in New York City, he sent a tape, dedicating that Mosque. The next day, I called him and thanked him for dedicating the Mosque, and he said, "O brother," in words, "that's not the mosque. One day brother, I'm going to build for you a mimbar." At that time, I didn't know what a mimbar was. But I did know what a mini-bar was.

I later learned that the mimbar was the place where the Kateeb delivers the khutbah. When he said to me, "One day I will build for you a mimbar, and it should have three steps." I didn't understand what he meant, but I think that I am beginning to understand it now. What he wanted to do was to move us gradually toward the perfection of the worship of Allah. He did not want us following that which had deviated from Allah and the Prophet.

Prophet Muhammad, peace be upon him, informed us that there would be three generations after him that would no longer be of him. He said, "The best of my people are my generation, then their immediate followers, then their immediate followers. After them there will be people who give false testimony without being asked, who will be treacherous and not be trusted, who will make vows which they do not fulfill, among whom fatness will appear."[8] The Prophet, peace be upon him, talked about the coming of the Mahdi out of his family. Now there is no need for a Mahdi or guide if you are already on the Path and know the way. It is clear that the world of the Muslims lost the way, otherwise they wouldn't be in the condition that they are in under the foot of the Western powers of unbelief (kufr).

---

[8]Reported by Imran b. Husain, transmitted by Bukhari and Muslim. See Mishkat al-Masaabih, p.1318

We have made our religion a religion of rituals, and the substance for which the Prophet, peace be upon him, lived and gave his life is no longer seen in the community of Muslims. We don't come to Islam to be a showboat Muslim, or to dress as an Arab or somebody else, and then act like somebody else. We are not to sit down and do nothing about our faith. If that is the kind of religion you want, then Islam is not what you want.

There are those who say, " Well Farrakhan, why are you so upset?" My response to them is to look at all of our people out there, dying due to the lack of knowledge. How many of them did we call to the Way of Allah? Whether you agree with the Honorable Elijah Muhammad or not, his whole program was to go after the people. You could tell him, "We raised a thousand dollars," [and] He [would] say, "How many Lost Founds (African-Americans) did you bring?" His aim was to bring the people out of where they were and start them in the process of coming back to Allah, coming back to themselves. Today we have no excuse for not doing the same thing because this country has given us the greatest opportunity to spread Islam.

In America can be found every race on the earth, and the only thing that will make them brothers to one another is Islam. The only thing that can save America from her moral degeneracy and fall is Islam. You and I know that the level of Christianity they have been given is powerless to reform them. Islam, transforms our lives. Take for example that when a baby cries, I don't care what the mother is doing, when she hears her baby, she answers the call of her child.

You could be in the most important meeting of your life, but when nature calls, what do you do? Do you sit there and keep going with the meeting or do you say, "Pardon me, just a moment. I have to be excused for just a moment." That's a call. You say that it is nature calling, but everybody answers nature's call.

When the mother is pregnant and it is time to give birth–she may have very important things to do, but when nature calls, she has to stop and lay down and give birth to that new life. Another example is that when it is time for us to leave this earthly plane, no matter what plans we have, when Allah Calls, we answer.

Well what about Allah's Call to us? Allah says in the Qur'an, "O you who believe, keep your duty to Allah as it ought to be kept, and die not unless you are Muslim."[9] Well what is this duty to Allah? His Call is greater than any other call. He and the Messenger has more rights over us than we have over ourselves, so when He calls, shouldn't we respond to the Call of God. If Allah has called us to Islam, called us to go after the people, and to submit our will to do His Will and to change our way of doing things, is there any call bigger than the Call of Allah?

This "Call" to the Prophet (pbuh) and to the believers as an obligation can best be understood when Allah says: "When My servants ask you concerning Me, I am indeed close [to them]. I listen to the prayer of every suppliant when he calls on Me. Let them also, with a will, listen to My Call and believe in Me–that they may walk in the right Way."[10]

I would like to say to all Muslims; we should always come to the Mosque with someone. We should not walk by people who are suffering, and not reach out to invite them to Islam when we know that Islam is the healing for all ills. Our whole life, as we live it as a Muslim–people look at us, and say, "They are different." There are times when some of them want to question us about our Faith. If we don't know our faith, how can we answer intelligently.

Islam is under attack all over the world. In America, Islam is under severe attack by a Zionist controlled media and a Zionist controlled government. Muslims must recognize that we have to settle our differences and come into some form of unity so that we can protect the entire Ummah of Muslims in America. If we fail to recognize that Islam is under assault, and think that everything is going to be alright, then we will continue to allow them to put in the movies and on television pictures that show our religion as a religion of terrorist or to show Muslims in a light that is far different from the reality of Islam. This happens and will continue to happen if we don't have an adequate response. Anytime

---

[9]Qur'an 2:132
[10]Qur'an 2:286

somebody criticizes a Jewish person, the Anti-Defamation League gets right on it. Muslims have to do likewise and defend our Faith.

There is a Reverend Price who comes on television every Sunday. He attacks Prophet Muhammad, peace be upon him, and his domestic life. He claims to have read over forty-two hundred (4200) hadith, and he reads them to defeat Islam. But the more he reads, the more he will see the beauty of Islam.

I don't pay any attention to his arguments because they are very weak. There may be some Muslims who may become angry with him and say, "See what that man Price is doing. Somebody ought to deal with him."

Wait a minute! When you start thinking violence, you've run out of arguments. Allah says in the Qur'an that He has given us the best argument. But how are you going to know the argument that God has given you if you won't read the Book. Every Muslim must be a student of the Qur'an and not allow some imams or some sheiks or anybody else to read for you. Read it for yourself. The command to the Prophet "Read," is a command to each one of us. Take your Qur'an down off the shelf and read it and become a student of the Word of Allah.

As I listened to Reverend Price, I said, "O, this man is helping Islam." He told his congregation, "You can't say anything if you haven't read it. I've read forty-two hundred hadiths. You can't say anything about Elijah Muhammad if you haven't read 'Message To The Blackman.' You can't say anything about the Qur'an unless you've read the Qur'an." Well let's get out there with our Qur'ans... Actually, what he is doing is opening the door for an intelligent, rational dialogue that is free of ego.

Let no Muslim ever think in terms of harming the man, because he is today like Paul who was a persecutor of Jesus until he was on the road to Damascus and had an experience. He's like Khalid bin-Walid who had a great sword–it's sharp, and he was using it against the Prophet, peace be upon him. But when a believer got next to him and presented him with the arguments of God, he became the sword of Allah.

Never, ever think of harming a person who is arguing with you on the basis of what they believe. Come back with your argument, and if you can't argue intelligently, the Book says, "Walk away nobly."

Before the new century comes in, I would like all of those Muslims who love and follow the Honorable Elijah Muhammad to become so knowledgeable of the Qur'an, of the Prophet of Islam, peace be upon him, and of his hadith, that you will be able to say with me that, "I believe that Elijah Muhammad followed the Sunnah of Prophet Muhammad, peace be upon him." I believe that I can prove to any scholar that he followed the Sunnah.

How did the Prophet act? And how did the Honorable Elijah Muhammad act. And see if there is a similarity between the Sunnah of the Prophet, and the practice of the Honorable Elijah Muhammad. There was no reason for Master Fard (teacher of the Honorable Elijah Muhammad) to have only one picture of himself. And in that only picture he is reading Qur'an. What was the lesson in that for his servant? Study the Qur'an. Why did he give him one hundred and four (104) books to study? And each one of these books had some aspect of the life of Prophet Muhammad, peace be upon him.

Why did he do that? Because the only way we are going to establish Islam in America is to look at the Sunnah of the Prophet, peace be upon him, who established Islam in Arabia and follow that Sunnah. Not just the dress, or the beard, or the miswak, or the camel, or the way he ate, etc. That was his practice of that time. The real Sunnah of the Prophet, peace be upon him, is how he practiced the Qur'an during the time of its revelation, and no ayat (verse) of this book was revealed outside of a context. The Qur'an has real value in context. And there is nothing happening in the world today that you cannot apply the Qur'an, and ayats (verses) from it to solve that problem. All we have to do is go back and look at how the Prophet, peace be upon him, acted.

I say to my dear beloved brothers and sisters. Elijah Muhammad is like a father to me. I can never be ungrateful to him for suffering. I don't know of no other black man in America who suffered so that somebody could say, "As-salaam-alaikum."

The Muhammad family wore the name Muhammad when the name Muhammad had no value in American society. But today, you can turn on your radio, and you have Jamal this, Kamal that, Karim this, Jabar that, etc. They didn't pay the price to wear that name like the family of Muhammad and the early followers who had Islamic names, such as Muhammad Ali and others. We can't discount that because that's part of our growing.

An analogy of our growth can be found in the Qur'an wherein Allah says, "I created you from sperm mixed with ovum." You are not that now. But why curse sperm? Why curse ovum when that is the base of your existence? He said, "And then a clot." Why curse a clot simply because it was ugly? It kept on evolving from a clot to an embryo, to a fetus, then to a baby that you could hold in your arms.

Well, what about how we grow Islamically. Since we say that Allah is Rabbil Alamin (Lord of all the worlds), and the One who starts creation, then causes it to grow stage after stage until it reaches its eventual perfection–how could we grow in America from a dead level, and not come through stages of evolution. You should never curse what you were. Keep on growing to your perfection of the manifestation of God?

May Allah, the Most High, bless Muslims throughout America and throughout the world. May Allah bless us to become a light that reflects the beauty of Islam; in our daily lives, in our family life, and in our community life.

Minister Louis Farrakhan

بِسْـــــمِ اللهِ الرَّحْمـٰنِ الرَّحِيمِ

In the Name of Allah,
The Beneficent, The Merciful

اَلصَّلَاةُ

Prayer

(Salat)[1]

"Prayer is the soul of religion. Where there is no prayer, there can be no purification of the soul. The non-praying person is rightly considered to be a person without a soul. Take prayer out of the world, and it is all over with religion because it is with prayer that man has the consciousness of God and selfless love for humanity and the inner sense of piety. Prayer is therefore, the first, the highest, and the most solemn phenomenon and mani-festation of religion.

"The way in which prayer is offered and the words which are recited in it explain the true nature of religion of which it is the expression of man's communication with his Lord.

"...The very first thing which comes into prominence in Islamic prayer is that it is accompanied by bodily movements. It implies that Islam lift not only the soul to the spiritual height, but also illuminates the body of the person with God-consciousness. It aims at purifying both body and soul, for it finds no cleavage between them. Islam does not regard body and soul as two differ-ent entities opposed to each other, or body as the prison of the soul from which it yearns to secure freedom in order to soar to heavenly heights. The soul is an organ of the body which exploits it for physiological purposes, and the body is an instrument of soul and both need spiritual enlightenment."[2]

---

[1] The word "Salat" means to pray, supplicate, to make petition or to perform the divinely appointed act. Salat in the technical sense means that particular mode of prayer which is enjoined upon the Muslims as a foremost religious duty.

[2] Imam Hamid Siddiqi, Sahih Muslim, vol. I, p. 206, Kitab Al-Salat, Introduction.

Prayer Purifies

We are told in the Qur'an that prayer keeps the Believer away from indecency and evil, provided one recites or obeys the guidance of the Qur'an and remembers Allah. This is stated in Surah Al-Ankabut (The Spider):

"Recite what has been revealed of the Book, and establish regular Prayer, surely prayer keeps (one) away from indecency and evil; and the remembrance of Allah is the greatest (thing in life) without doubt. And Allah knows what you do."[3]

Many times we may have heard the phrase repeated, "Surely prayer keeps (one) away from indecency and evil..." Even though this is true, there are other aspects related to prayer that are essential if we are to receive the full benefits from our prayers.

In the above verse, Allah not only ask us to pray on a regular basis, He also tells us to recite the Qur'an and to remember Him. Thus, there are three facets mentioned here that gives us protection against evil and indecency. It is the combination of these three essentials that we must incorporate in our daily life, of which the recitation of the Qur'an is the most essential. Imam Maududi in explaining the need to recite the Qur'an states:

"Now that we are being told to recite the Qur'an and establish the Salat (Prayer) as a practical device, for these are the two things which endow a believer with a strong character and wonderful capacity by which he can not only brave successfully the most violent storms of evil and falsehood, but can even subdue them.

"Man can acquire this power from the recitation of the Qur'an and the Prayer only when he does not remain content with the mere recital of the words but also understands well the Qur'anic teachings and absorbs them in his soul, and his prayer does not remain confined to physical movements but becomes the very function of his heart and the motive force for his morals and character... As for its recitation, one should know that the recitation which does not reach the heart beyond the throat, cannot even

---
[3]Qur'an 29:45

give man enough power to remain steadfast to his faith, not to speak of enabling him to withstand the furies of disbelief. About such people, Prophet Muhammad ﷺ said:

"They will recite the Qur'an, but the Qur'an will not go beyond their throats. They will leave the Faith just as the arrow leaves the bow."[4]

Bukhari and Muslim

"He whose Prayer did not restrain him from the evil and indecent acts, offered no Prayer at all."[5]

"The recitation (of the Qur'an) that does not effect any change in a person's way of thinking and a person's morals and character, and that person goes on doing what the Qur'an forbids, is not the recitation of a Believer... Such a recitation does not reform and strengthen a person's self and spirit, but makes such a person more stubborn against Allah and impudent before one's own conscience and destroys their character...

"For the person who believes in the Qur'an as a Divine Book, reads it and comes to know what his God has enjoined, and then goes on violating His injunctions, is of the culprit, who commits a crime not due to ignorance, but after full knowledge of the law. Prophet Muhammad ﷺ has elucidated this point in a brief sentence, thus:

"The Qur'an is a testimony in your favor as well as against you."[6]

"If you follow the Qur'an rightly, it is a testimony in your favor. Whenever you are called to account for your deeds, here or in the Hereafter, you can produce the Qur'an as a testimony in your defence, saying that whatever you did was in accordance with this Book... If this Book has reached you, and you have read it and found out what your Lord demands from you, what He enjoins and what He forbids, and then you adopt an attitude opposed to it, then this Book will be a testimony against you. It will further strengthen the criminal case against you in the Court of Allah. Then it will in no way be possible for you to escape the

---

[4]Bukhari and Muslim.

[5] Reported by Ibn Abi Hatim.

[6] Muslim, Vol. I, pp. 147, 148, No. 432.

punishment or receive a light punishment by making the excuse of ignorance."[7]

When we are told in this same verse that the "remembrance of Allah is the Greatest thing in life without doubt," we must understand how this applies to our life. Imam Maududi also give a good comment as to how we are to understand this in its proper context.

"...The remembrance of Allah... not only restrains from the evils, but over and above that, it induces one to act righteously and urges one to excel in good acts. When a person observes a fast or pays the Zakat or performs a righteous act, that person inevitably remembers Allah. That is why the righteous act emanates from such a person. Likewise, when a person refrains from an evil act when an opportunity to do so presents itself, this also is the result of Allah's remembrance. Therefore, the remembrance of Allah pervades the entire life of the believer."[8]

From the above, we learn that Prayer alone is not enough if we are ignorant to our Religion Islam and what it demands of us. Living in a corrupt society can have an enormous impact on our daily life. Our only protection against the evils is that we know what Allah has given to us as guidance (Qur'an), and a constant remembrance of Him to keep us on a path that is pleasing to Him. We do not want to put ourselves in the position of one whom Allah says is unmindful of his or her prayers.

"Woe to the worshippers who are unmindful of their prayers, who pray to be seen, but refuse (to supply even) neighborly needs."[9]

The importance of prayer in Islam can be found in Surah Nur (Light). If Muslims are to once again find favor with Allah, and regain the glory of Islam, then prayer is an essential element that must be performed community-wise, and in the context that Islam has prescribed for the believers, and not as just an individual obligation as many Muslims assume today.

[7] Imam Abul A'la Maududi, The Meaning of the Qur'an, Vol. IX, Note 77, pp. 162, 163.
[8] Imam Abu A'la Maududi, The Meaning of the Qur'an, vol. IX, Note 79, p. 166.
[9] Qur'an 107:4-7.

Prophet Muhammad 鷺 has made it clear of the importance of prayer when he 鷺 said,

"Verily, between man and polytheism and disbelief is the negligence of prayer."[9a]

"Abdullah b. Masad said that he asked the Messenger of Allah 鷺 which deed was best, and he 鷺 replied, 'Prayer at its appointed hour.' I again asked what then, and he 鷺 replied, 'Kindness to parents.' I then asked, what then, and he 鷺 replied, 'Jihad in the Cause of Allah.'"[9b]

In Surah Nur, Allah says:

"Allah has promised to those among you who believe and work righteous deeds, that He will of a surety grant them in the land, inheritance (of power), as He granted it to those before them, that He will establish in authority their religion (Way of Life-Din), the one which He has chosen for them, and that He will change (their state) after the fear in which they (lived), to one of security and peace. They will worship Me (alone) and not associate aught with Me. If any do reject Faith after this, they are rebellious and wicked.

"So establish regular prayer, and give regular charity, and obey the Messenger that you may receive mercy." Qur'an 25:55-56

[9a]Reported by Abu Hurairah, transmitted by Muslim, Vol. I, p. 48, no. 146.
[9b]Transmitted by Muslim, Vol. I, pp. 49-50, nos. 148-153.

بسم الله الرحمن الرحيم

In the Name of Allah,
The Beneficent, The Merciful

Times of Prayer

"When you pass (Congregational) prayers, celebrate
Allah's praises, standing, sitting down, or lying down
on your sides; but when you are free from danger, set up
regular Prayers, for such prayers are enjoined on Be-
lievers at stated times."   Qur'an 4:103

The performance of prayer is obligatory on every Muslim who attains the age of discretion. Muslims must offer the obligatory (fard) prayers when they are due unless unusual circumstances prevent one from doing so. If such a situation occurs that one is unable to perform the obligatory (fard) prayer during its time period, it must be made up as soon as possible. If one is able to offer the obligatory (fard) prayer at its prescribed time, but fails to do so, they are committing a sin.

Anyone who misses an obligatory prayer must make it up with the exception of women in confinement (childbirth), women who are experiencing their menstrual cycle, or people who are insane or unconscious.

Making up missed obligatory prayers must be within 24 hours of their regular time, even if the sun is rising or setting. One is not obligated to offer the sunnah (voluntary/tradition) prayer when making up the obligatory prayer. For example, If one gets up late for the Dawn (Fajr) prayer, it should be offered even though the sun is rising. Any prayer that has been missed should not be offered before a prayer that is due unless sufficient time remains for the completion of both. If one missed the Noon (Zuhr) prayer, and there is only enough time to offer the Afternoon (Asr) before the sun sets, then the Noon (Zuhr) prayer should be offered before performing the Evening (Maghrib) prayer.

If more than one prayer has been missed, they may all be offered one after the other. When making up for the missed prayers, only the Iqamah is said before each prayer, and not the Adhan. When making up for the missed prayer, one should say before each prayer missed:

"I intend to offer the missed obligatory (name of prayer) to Allah, the Most High."

The Obligatory Prayers

The following is a listing of the five obligatory prayers and the times when they are due. Also listed is the pronunciation of their names in Arabic and their names as translated into English:

1. **Fajr (Early Morning prayer).** This is the first obligatory prayer of the day, and it is said after dawn and before sunrise. If one gets up late, then the prayer may be offered even though the sun has risen. This prayer consist of two rakahs, and is recited audibly. If one has missed this prayer, it should not be said during the first thirty minutes after the sun has risen.

2. **Zuhr (Early Afternoon prayer).** This is the second obligatory prayer of the day, and it is said when the sun begins to decline (passed it zenith) , and its time extends until the Asr or Afternoon prayer. This prayer consist of four rak'ahs which are recited silently.

3. **'Asr (Afternoon prayer).** This is the third obligatory prayer, and it is said when the sun is about midway on its course to setting, and its time extends until the sun begins to set. The saying of this prayer at its prescribed time is so important, that its importance is mentioned in the Qur'an as well as in the traditions (hadith). This prayer consist of four rak'ahs which are recited silently.

4. **Maghrib (Sunset prayer).** This is the fourth obligatory prayer, and it is said immediately after the sun has set, and its time extends until the red glow in the west disapperars. This prayer consist of three rak'ahs, the first two rak'ahs being recited audibly, and the third rak'ah silently.

5. 'Isha' (Night prayer). This is the fifth and last obligatory prayer, and it is said after the red glow in the west disappears, and its time extends until midnight. This prayer should be offered just before one goes to bed so that it is the last act of the day. This prayer consists of four rak'ahs, the first two rak'ahs are recited audibly, the last two rak'ahs are recited silently.

Sunnah Prayers (Voluntary)

1. Fajr (Early Morning prayer). Two rak'ahs of sunnah prayer offered before the saying of the Fajr prayer, which are offered silently, as is the case with all sunnah prayers.

2. Zuhr (Early Afternoon prayer). Two or four rak'ahs of sunnah prayer offered before saying the Zuhr prayer, and two after.

3. 'Asr (Afternoon prayer). Four rak'ahs (optional) of sunnah prayer offered before saying the 'Asr prayer.

4. Maghrib (Sunset prayer). Two rak'ahs of sunnah prayer offered after saying the Maghrib prayer.

5. 'Isha' (Night prayer). Four rak'ahs of sunnah prayer after the 'Isha' prayer, followed by three rak'ahs called witr.[10] The three rak'ahs of Shaf"il Witr are said audibly.

Obligatory (Fard) and Traditional (Sunnah) Prayers

Name of Prayer:	Obligatory part: No. of rak'ahs Fard	Traditional part: No. of rak'ahs Before Fard	After Fard
FAJR (Early Morning Prayer)	2	2	
ZUHR (Early Afternoon Prayer)	4	2 or 4	2
'ASR (Afternoon Prayer)	4	none 2 or 4	
MAGHRIB (Sunset Prayer)	3		2
'ISHA' (Night Prayer)	4		4 + 3 witr*

*This is the Witr prayer that consists of 3 rak'ahs following the traditional (Sunnah) part of the 'Isha' (Night) prayer.

---

[10] More information on how to perform the witr prayer can best be obtained from your Imam, from Muslims who know how to perform it, or from books on the subject of prayer in Islam.

بسم الله الرحمن الرحيم

In the Name of Allah,
The Beneficent, The Merciful

Ablution
(Wudu)

"O you who believe. When you prepare for
prayer, wash your faces and your hands (and arms) to
the elbows. Rub your heads (with water), and (wash)
your feet to the ankles. If you are in a state of ceremo-
nial impurity, bathe your whole body. But if you are ill
or on a journey, or one of you come from offices of na-
ture, or you have been in contact with women and you
cannot find water, then take for yourselves clean sand
or earth, and rub therewith your faces and hands.
Allah does not wish to place you in difficulty, but to
make you clean, and to complete His Favor to you
that you may be grateful." **Qur'an 5:7**

The above verse from the Qur'an fairly sums up how one is to make ablution (wudu) or tayammum, and the conditions for which they are to be performed.

When the Qur'an speaks of taking clean earth or sand cleaning one's self for prayer, it is addressing how one is to perform tayammum which under certain conditions can be done in place of taking ablution (wudu). Tayammum is performed simply by taking clean earth or sand, and passing it over the face and hands only.

Tayammum consists in striking both hands on pure earth or anything containing pure dust, then blowing off the excess of dust from the hands and passing the hands over the face and the backs of the two hands, the left over the right and the right over the left.

When a person is sick or when clean water is not available, tayammum is to be performed in place of wudu (ablution) or ghusl (complete bath)

The word "wudu" which has been translated into English as "ablution" can best be described as the process of cleaning those parts of the body which are generally exposed. The word "wudu" itself is derived from the Arabic word "wadza" which means beauty.

In addressing the performance of wudu (ablution), we find in the tradition (hadith) greater details on how it is to be performed, just as we find in the tradition (hadith), how the prayer in detail is to be performed.

The practice of Prophet Muhammad 饔 in the tradition in performing the ablution is similar in detail.

Before you begin the ablution, state your intention (niyyah) to make ablution by reciting:

"I am about to make my ablution for Allah, the Lord and Cherisher of all the worlds."

Then recite the following:

بِسْـمِ اللّٰهِ الرَّحْـمٰنِ الرَّجِيْمِ

Bismillah ar-Rahman nir-Rahim
(In the Name of Allah, the Beneficent, The Merciful)

Then begin the ablution, which is as follows:

1.   The hands are washed three times up to the wrist, the right hand first, then the left hand. The hands should be rubbed allowing water to reach between the fingers.

2.   The mouth is cleaned with water by rinsing three times with fresh water. It is preferable to brush the teeth before prayer.

3.   The nostrils are cleaned three times by snuffing a little water into the right one first, then the left or by snuffing water into both of them at the same time, then blowing the nose if necessary.

4.   The face is washed three times from the top of the forehead to under the chin, and from ear to ear.

5.   The arms are washed three times from the wrist to the

elbows, beginning with the right arm and then the left arm.

6. The head is wiped over once from the top of the fore-head down to the neck, using three fingers of both hands, then the ears are washed simultaneously–the inner side of the ears wiped with forefingers and its outer side with the thumbs.

7. The feet are washed three times up to and including the ankles, beginning with the right foot, then the left foot. Water is to penetrate between the toes when washing.

If socks, stockings or shoes are being worn, and they have been put on after the feet have been washed, it is permissible to wipe over them with wet fingers. It is necessary however that the feet be washed at least once in every twenty-four hour period. If the socks or the shoes are taken off, the ablution is still in effect. If one is wearing shoes, they should be removed if the prayer is performed in the masjid.

Upon completion of ablution, one should recite the following:

أَشْهَدُ أَنْ لَآ إِلَهَ إِلَّا اللهُ

Ashhadu anla e-laha ill-Allahu
(I bear witness that there is no god except Allah.)

وَأَشْهَدُ أَنَّ مُحَمَّدًا عَبْدُهُ وَرَسُولُهُ ·

Wa ashhadu anna Muhammadan 'abduhu wa rasulluh.
(And I bear witness that Muhammad is His Servant and Messenger.)

Prophet Muhammad ﷺ is reported to have said that the one who recites the above supplication after the ablution, "The eight gates of Paradise would be opened for him and he may enter by whichever of them he wishes."[11]

Ablution may be performed before every prayer, but the necessity for it arises only when there has been a violation that void the ablution.

Acts which invalidate or nullify the ablution

1. There has been a natural evacuation of any solid, liquid from the anus or genitals. In such case, wherever the evacuation

---

[11] Reported by 'Uqba b. 'Amir, Sahih Muslim, p. 152, nos. 451, 452.

has taken place, that part of the body must be wiped and cleaned with water.

    a.   In the case of those who are afflicted with a condition of permanent wetting, their ablution is not broken even though it occurs during prayer. In such a case, the person should repeat the ablution before every prayer.

    2.   Emission of semen during sleep or while one is awake, ablution and total bath (Ghusl)[12] becomes obligatory.

    3.   Touching of the sexual organs intentionally, directly and unclothed.

    4.   Sleeping, no matter what the circumstances. If one is sitting down in the masjid waiting for prayer and is overcome by drowsiness, in such case the ablution is not invalidated.

    5.   Vomiting.

    6.   Temporary insanity, fainting or hysteria.

    7.   Women with an emission of blood or secretion.[13]

    8.   Deliberately touching a woman for reasons of lust.

When a complete bath becomes obligatory

    1.   After the ejaculation of semen due to a sexual act or even the thought of it.

    2.   After sexual intercourse even though there is no orgasm.

    3.   Following a dream by a man or woman of an erotic nature if the dreamer should find any trace of semen on his clothes or bed. However, should the person see in their dream that which would require total ablution, yet on waking find no trace on their clothes or bed, then it is not required to carry out a complete bath (Ghusl).

    4.   Following menstruation of a woman.

    5.   At the end of forty days after childbirth. If the hemorrhaging of childbirth ceases before forty days, the woman may carry out a complete bath (Ghusl). There is no requirement that forty days must elapse.

---

[12] Ghusl is the total washing of the whole body, which is the pouring of water over the whole body from the head to the feet.

[13] Women are not permitted to fast or offer obligatory (fard) prayers during their menstrual cycle. Upon completion of the menstrual cycle an obligatory bath (ghusl) become necessary.

6. When a new convert accepts Islam, such a person should be instructed to carry out a complete bath (Ghusl) following his or her proclamation (shahadah) of acceptance.

How to perform a complete bath (Ghusl)

To perform a complete bath (Ghusl), clean water must be used throughout the process to wash the body. If a shower is available, it is permissible to use it. One is not allowed to bathe in a tub of standing water where dirt or scum can accumulate during the cleaning process. If bathing in a tub, the water must be clean and poured over the body during the cleaning process, and the used water allowed to drain from the tub.

To begin the process of a complete bath (Ghusl), one should make the intention to clean the body of impurities, reciting silently or audibly, and then say:

بِسْمِ اللهِ الرَّحْمٰنِ الرَّحِيْمِ

Bismillah ar-Rahman, nir-Rahim
(In the Name of Allah, The Beneficent, The Merciful).

1. One should wash the hands, beginning with the right hand first.
2. After washing the hands, one should clean their private parts with their left hand.
3. After cleaning the private parts, one should perform the ritual of ablution (wudu) with the exception that the feet should be left until the rest of the body has been washed.
4. After the ablution (wudu), wash the hair, making certain that the water touches the roots (scalp).
5. With the exception of the private parts which have already been washed, the entire body is then washed and cleaned of any impurities, washing the legs and feet last.

بِسْمِ اللهِ الرَّحْمٰنِ الرَّحِيمِ

In the Name of Allah,
The Beneficent, The Merciful

اَلْأَذَانُ
Adhan
(Announcement)

The Adhan is the "Call to Prayer" which is made before every congregational prayer service. It is in the Adhan that we find the teachings of the Qur'an and Sunnah beautifully summed up. If a person were to listen to nothing but the Adhan and grasp its meaning, he could understand all the essentials of the Faith. The main purpose behind the pronouncement five times a day is to make available to everyone an easily intelligible brief version of Islam.

When announcing the Adhan, the Caller (Mu'adhdhin) assumes the standing position and raises his hands to his ears. (See Illustration, page 30) With hands cupped, palms forward and thumbs under his ear lobes, he makes the following announcement in a loud, chanting voice:

أَللهُ أَكْبَرُ ، أَللهُ أَكْبَرُ

Allahu Akbar, Allahu Akbar
Allah is The Greatest, Allah is The Greatest

أَللهُ أَكْبَرُ ، أَللهُ أَكْبَرُ

Allahu Akbar, Allahu Akbar
Allah is The Greatest, Allah is The Greatest

أَشْهَدُ أَنْ لَا إِلٰهَ إِلاَّ اللهُ

Ash-had-do anla ila-ha il-lal-lah
I bear witness that there is no god except Allah

أَشْهَدُ أَنْ لَا إِلٰهَ إِلاَّ اللهُ

Ash-had-do anla ila-ha il-lal-lah
I bear witness that there is no god except Allah

أَشْهَدُ أَنْ مُحَمَّدًا رَسُولُ الله

Ash-had-do anna Muhamma-dar Ra-su-lul-lah
I bear witness that Muhammad is the Messenger of Allah

أَشْهَدُ أَنْ مُحَمَّدًا رَسُولُ الله

Ash-had-do anna Muhamma-dar Ra-su-lul-lah
I bear witness that Muhammad is the Messenger of Allah

(Turning the head to the right, announce)

حَيَّ عَلَى الصَّلاة ، حَيَّ عَلَى الصَّلاة

Hay-ya 'alas sa-lah, Hay-ya 'alas sa-lah
Come to prayer, Come to prayer

(Turning the head to the left, announce)

حَيَّ عَلَى الْفَلاح ، حَيَّ عَلَى الفَلاح

Hay-ya 'alal fa-lah, hay-ya 'alal fa-lah
Come to success, come to success

(Turning the head once again in the direction of the Ka'bah, announce)

أَللهُ أَكْبَر ، أَللهُ أَكْبَر

Allahu Akbar, Allahu Akbar
Allah is the Greatest, Allah is the Greatest

لا إِلٰهَ إِلاَّ الله

La ila-ha il-lal-lah.
There is no god except Allah.

For the Morning (Fajr) prayer only, after the Caller says, "Hayya 'alal-falah," the following words are said:

أَلصَّلاةُ خَيْرٌ مِنَ النَّوْمِ

As-salatu khai-rum minan naum
Prayer is better than sleep

أَلصَّلاةُ خَيْرٌ مِنَ النَّوْمِ

As-salatu khai-rum min-nan naum
Prayer is better than sleep

After the Caller has finished the First Call, he and the followers may offer the following prayer:

أَللّٰهُمَّ رَبَّ هٰذِهِ الدَّعْوَةِ الْتَامَّةِ وَالصَّلاةِ القَائِمَةِ

*Allah-hum-ma Rabba hathi-hid-da 'wa-tit-tammati,
was-sala-til-qa- 'imati*
O Allah, Lord of this perfect call and the prayer to be offered.

آتِ مُحَمَّدًا الوَسِيلَةَ وَالفَضِيلَةَ

Ati Muhamma-da-nil wasilata wal-fadilata
Grant Muhammad the way of approach to You and also the eminence.

وَابْعَثْهُ مَقَامًا

wab 'ath-hu maqaman
And elevate him to the glorious position which You have promised him,

مَحْمُودًا الَّذِي وَعَدْته

mahmuda nil-lathi wa 'at-tah
And afford us his intercession on the Day of Judgment,

إِنَّكَ لا تُخْلِفُ الْمِيعَاد

innaka la tukhliful mi'aad
for You never go back on Your Promise.

When the Adhan is announced, every Muslim must prepare for prayer. Upon hearing it, a Muslim should make every effort to join the congregational prayer. It is recommended that the listener repeat the words of the Adhan after the Caller.

بِسْـــمِ اللهِ الرَّحْمَنِ الرَّحِيمِ

In the Name of Allah,
The Beneficent, The Merciful

اَلْإِقَامَةُ

Iqamah

The Iqamah is to be announced just before the Imam begins the congregational prayer. It is said to announce the commencement of the congregational prayer.

After the Caller has made the Adhan, there should be an interval before the Iqamah is announced, during which time a Muslim prepares for the prayer service. If one is eating, they should have enough time to finish their food, to make ablution and have enough time to get to the masjid and offer the Sunnah prayers. Prophet Muhammad ﷺ said, "There is a prayer between the two Adhans (Adhan and Iqamah) for whoever wants to pray."[14]

The interval between the Adhan and Iqamah should allow at least sufficient time to finish a meal (if one is eating), make ablution, go to the masjid and perform sunnah prayer.

The words of the Iqamah should be said in a lower tone of voice and delivered with quickness. The person who makes the Adhan is generally the one who announces the Iqamah, however it is acceptable for someone else to make the Iqamah. Anas bin Malik reported, "Bilal was ordered to pronounce the wording of Adhan twice, and that of the Iqamah once, with the exception of 'Qad qamatis salat (Prayer is commencing).'"[15] The Iqamah is said as follows:

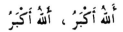

Allahu Akbar, Allahu Akbar
Allah is The Greatest, Allah is The Greatest

---

[14] Bukhari, Vol. I, p. 342, nos. 596 and 597.
[15] Bukhari, Vol. I, p. 335, no. 580.

أَشْهَدُ أَنْ لاَ إِلَٰهَ إِلاَّ الله

Ash-had-do anla ila-ha il-lal-lah

I bear witness that there is no god except Allah

أَشْهَدُ أَنَّ مُحَمَّدًا رَسُولُ الله

Ash-had-do anna Muhamma-dar Ra-su-lul-lah

I bear witness that Muhammad is the Messenger of Allah

حَيَّ عَلَى الصَّلاة

Hay-ya 'alas sa-lah

Come to prayer

حَيَّ عَلَى الْفَلاح

Hay-ya 'alal fa-lah

Come to success

قَدْ قَامَتِ الصَّلاةُ ، قَدْ قَامَتِ الصَّلاةُ

Qad qa-ma-tis-salatu, qad qa-ma-tis-salah

Prayer is commencing, prayer is commencing

أللهُ أَكْبَرُ ، أللهُ أَكْبَر

Allahu Akbar, Allahu Akbar

Allah is The Greatest, Allah is The Greatest.

لاَ إِلَٰهَ إِلاَّ الله

La ila-ha il-lal-lah.

There is no God except Allah.

When making the Iqamah, both hands remain at the sides as in the standing position. (See Illustration, page 29) The face is not turned to the right or left when announcing "Come to prayer (Hayya 'alas-salah)," or "Come to success (Hayya 'alal-falah)." The Caller announces, "Prayer is commencing (Qad qama-tis-salah)" to alert the congregation that prayer is about to begin. At this point, the congregation stands and forms straight lines for the prayer service.

Should the Imam be standing when the Iqamah is announced, the members of the congregation are permitted to stand also. If the Imam is sitting during the announcement of the Iqamah, then the members of the congregation should remain sitting until the Caller announces, "Prayer is commencing (Qad qama-tis-salah)".

بِسْــمِ اللهِ الرَّحْمٰنِ الرَّحِيمِ

In the Name of Allah,
The Beneficent, The Merciful

Performance of Prayer

When teaching one of his followers how to pray, Prophet Muhammad ﷺ instructed, "When you stand for prayer say, 'Allah is the Greatest,' then recite from the Holy Qur'an some of that which you know by heart, then bow till you feel at ease. Then raise your head and stand up straight, then prostrate until you feel at ease during your prostration, then sit with calmness until you feel at ease [do not hurry], and do the same in all your prayers."[16] Prophet Muhammad ﷺ also said:

"Whoever does not recite Al-Fatiha in his prayer, his prayer is invalid."[17]

The prayer service begins by standing and facing in the direction of the Ka'bah which is in the Holy City Mecca. Here in America we turn in a northeasterly direction to face the Ka'bah. In different countries, the direction of the Ka'bah varies. Those living in other parts of the world, such as China, India, Pakistan and other countries in the East turn their faces toward the west, while those in Russia turn their faces southwest. Muslims in Britain and neighboring countries turn their faces towards the southeast, etc.

Pages 29-57 give detailed instructions and illustrations on how to perform two, three and four Steps (Rak'ahs).

---

[16]Bukhari, Vol. I, pp. 404-05, no. 724.
[17]Bukhari, Vol. I, p. 404, no. 723.

بســـــم االله الرحمـر الرحيـم

In the Name of Allah,
The Beneficent, The Merciful

PRAYER
ILLUSTRATIONS
AND
INSTRUCTIONS

"When the son of Adam recites the verse (ayat) of prostration (sajdah), and then falls down in prostration, Satan goes into seclusion and weeps and says, ' Alas, woe unto me, the son of Adam was commanded to prostrate and he prostrated and Paradise was entitled to him, and I was was commanded to prostrate, but I refused and am doomed to Hell.'"

—Prophet Muhammad

بســـم الله الرحمن الرحيم

In the Name of Allah,
The Beneficent, The Merciful

Prayer Service
for Performing Two, Three
and Four Rak'ahs

STEP 1 through STEP 18

Nawaitu an ussal-li Salatul-Fajr
ta buda'llahi ta'ala
I intend to perform the Morning prayer
as ordered by Allah, the Exalted

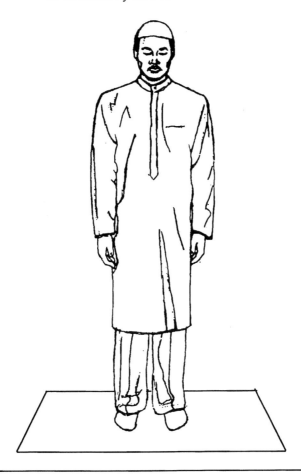

Instructions: Facing in the direction of the Ka'bah (Qiblah), standing up-right (qiyam position) with head slightly bowed, eyes focused on the spot where the forehead will rest during prostration, with arms at the sides. The feet are placed in a natural position with the distance between them approximately the width of the body. In the above posture, silently say your intention (niyyah) for the obligatory prayer you are about to perform.

Note: The above intention is for the Morning obligatory prayer (Salatul-Fajr), which consists of two rak'ahs.

STEP 2

أَللهُ أَكْبَر

Allahu Akbar
Allah is The Greatest

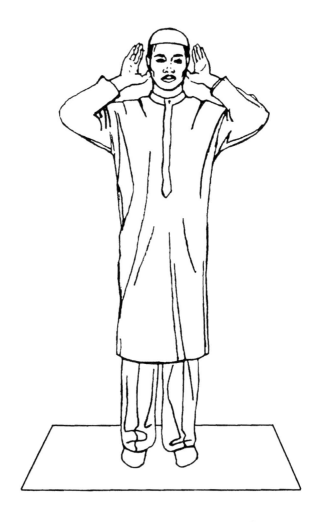

Instructions: After stating your intention (niyyah), remain in the standing position, raising both hands to the ears, palms forward, placing the thumbs under the ear lobes. Glorify Allah audibly, saying Takabiratul-Ihram as stated above.

Instructions: While still in the upright (Qiyam) position, the right hand is placed over the left, a little lower than the breast or just above the navel with the right hand slightly grasping the left wrist. Recite (Thana'), followed by Ta'awwuz, Tasmiyah and Al-Fatiha as stated on the following page.

STEP 3 (Continued)

سُبْحـانَكَ الـلـهُمَّ وَبِـحَمْدِكَ

Subhanak Allahumma wa bi-hamdika.
Pure and glorified are You, O Allah.

وَتَـبـارَكَ اسْمُكَ وَتَـعـالى جَدُّكَ

wa tabarakas muka wa ta'ala jadduka,
Blessed is Your Name, and exalted is Your Majesty,

ولا إلـهَ غَيْرُك

wa la elaaha ghai-ruk
and there is nothing worthy of worship except You.[1]

أَعوذُ بـاللهِ مِنَ الـشَّيْطانِ الـرَّجيم

A'oothu billaahee minash shaytaanir-rajeem.
I seek refuge with Allah from Satan, the accursed.[2]

بِـسْم اللّه

Bismillahir
In the Name of Allah,[3]

الـرَّخْمنِ الـرَّحيم

Rahman nir-Raheem.
The Beneficent, The Merciful.

أَلْـحَمْدُ لِـلَّهِ رَبِّ الـعـالَـمِين .

Al-hamdu lillahi Rabbil-'alamin;[4]
Praise be to Allah, the Lord of all the worlds;

---

[1] Thana'.
[2] Ta'awwuz.
[3] Tasmiyah or Basmala.
[4] Al-Fatiha (The Opening)

STEP 3 (Continued)

• أَلـرَّحْمـنِ الـرَّحِيـم

Ar-Rahman nir-Raheem.
The Beneficent, The Merciful.[1]

• مَـالِـكِ يَـوْم الـدِّيـن

Maliki yaum mid-deen.
Master of the Day of Judgment.

• إِيَّـاكَ نَـعْبُـدُ وَ إِيَّـاكَ نَـسْتَعِين

Iyyaka na'budu, wa iyyaka nasta'een
You do we worship, and Your Aid we seek.

• إِهْدِنَـا الـصِّرَاطَ الـمُسْتَقِيـم

ihdenas-seraa-tal mustaqeem,
Guide us on the straight way,

• صِرَاطَ الَّـذِيـنَ أَنْعَمْتَ عَلَيْـهِم

Siraatal latheena, an'amta 'alay-him,
the way of those on whom You have bestowed Your Grace,

• غَيْـرِ الـمَغْضُوبِ عَلَيْـهِم

Ghay-ril maghdoobee 'alay-him,
Those whose [portion] is not wrath,

• وَلا الـضَّـالِّيـن

Walad daaleen.
and who go not astray.

• آمِـين

Ameen.
Amin

---

[1]Al-Fatiha (The Opening), continued from page 32.

STEP 3 (Continued)

بِسْم اللّه

Bismillahir,
In the Name of Allah,[1]

الـرَّحْمنِ الـرَّحيم

Ar-Rahman nir-Raheem.
The Beneficent, The Merciful.

قُـلْ هُوَ اللّهُ أَحَدُ

Qul huwa Allahu Ahad.
Say: He is Allah, the One and Only.[2]

اللّهُ الـصَّمَـدُ

Allahu hus Samad;
Allah The Eternal, Absolute;

لَـمْ يَـلِـدْ وَلَـمْ يُولَـدْ

Lam yalid wa lam yulad,
He begets not, nor is he begotten,

وَلَـمْ يَكُنْ لَـهُ كُفُـوُا أَحَد

wa lam yakul lahu kufuwan Ahad.
and there is none like unto Him.

اللّهُ أَكْبَـر

Allahu Akbar.
Allah is the Greatest.[3]

---

[1]Tasmiyah.
[2]Al-Ikhlas (The Unity).
[3]Takbir
    Note: When one says Takbir (Allahu Akbar), it is a signal for a change of position.

STEP 3- (Continued)

Instructions: The standing (Qiyam) position for women is similar to that for men, as shown in STEP 3, page 35 (Qiyam). The only difference is that a woman folds her hands on her breast, not on or above her navel.

STEP 4

سُبْحـانَ رَبِّيَ الْـعَظِيم

Subhana Rabbiyal 'atheem.
Highly glorified is my Lord, The Mighty.

سُبْحـانَ رَبِّيَ الْـعَظِيم

Subhana Rabbiyal 'atheem.
Highly glorified is my Lord, The Mighty.

سُبْحـانَ رَبِّيَ الْـعَظِيم

Subhana Rabbiyal 'atheem.
Highly glorified is my Lord, The Mighty.

Instructions: Assume the bending (ruku') position by bending forward until the back is parallel with the floor, and placing the hands on the knees. While in this position looking straight down, glorify Allah (Tasbih) by reciting the above 3 times.

STEP 5

سَمِعَ اللهُ لِمَنْ حَمِده

Samee' Allahu liman hamidah.

Allah hears who praise Him.

رَبَّنا وَلَكَ الْحَمْدُ

Rabbana wa lakal hamd.

Our Lord, and for You is the praise.

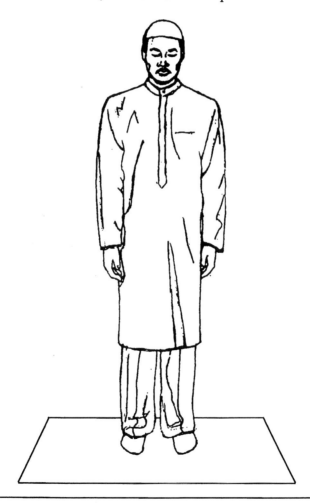

Instructions: While reciting the above, rise slowly from the bending (ruku')
position to an upright position.

STEP 5 (Continued)

الله أكْبَـر

Allahu Akbar
Allah is The Greatest

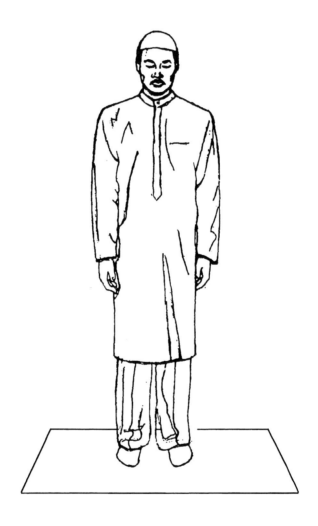

Instructions: After rising from the bending (ruku') position, say Takbir (Allahu-Akbar) as stated above.

سُبْحـانَ رَبِّيَ الأَغْلى

Subhana Rabbiyal A'ala.
Highly glorified is my Lord, The Most High.

سُبْحـانَ رَبِّيَ الأَغْلى

Subhana Rabbiyal A'ala.
Highly glorified is my Lord, The Most High.

سُبْحـانَ رَبِّيَ الأَغْلى

Subhana Rabbiyal A'ala.
Highly glorified is my Lord, The Most High.

اللهُ أَكْبَر

Allahu Akbar.
Allah is the Greatest.

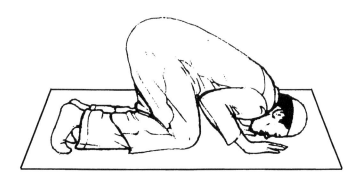

Instructions: Assume the prostrate (sajdah) position. The toes of both feet, both knees, both hands, forehead and nose touching the floor, with the elbows raised, and the head between the hands with fingers extended, and with the thumbs in line with the ears, recite the above 3 times and while rising, say takbir once. See page 58 for side view of sajdah for women.

STEP 7

اللهُمَّ اغْفِرْ لِي وَارْحَمْنِي

Allahumma-ghfirlee war-hamnee.
O Allah, pardon me and have mercy on me.

الله أَكْبَر

Allahu Akbar.
Allah is the Greatest.

Instructions: After prostrating, rise to the sitting (jalsah) position. After rising, say the above to yourself. Sit erect while in this position unless you are physically unable to do so.

Note: See page 56, STEP 16 for rearview position of jalsah or qa'dah.

سُبْحَانَ رَبِّيَ الأَغْلَى

Subhana Rabbiyal A'ala.

Highly glorified is my Lord, The Most High.

سُبْحَانَ رَبِّيَ الأَغْلَى

Subhana Rabbiyal A'ala.

Highly glorified is my Lord, The Most High.

سُبْحَانَ رَبِّيَ الأَغْلَى

Subhana Rabbiyal A'ala.

Highly glorified is my Lord, The Most High.

اللهُ أَكْبَر

Allahu Akbar.

Allah is the Greatest.

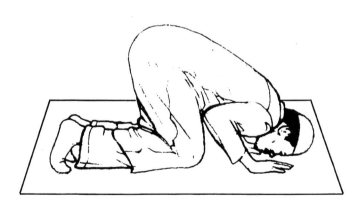

Instructions: Return to the prostrate (sajdah) position and recite the above Tasbih 3 times, and Takbir once.

Note: This completes one rak'ah.

STEP 9

بِسْمِ اللهِ الـرَّحْمنِ الـرَّحيم

Bismillahir, Rahman nir-Raheem.
In the Name of Allah, The Beneficent, The Merciful

Instructions: This begins the second Rak'ah. Recite once again Al-Fatiha (The Opening Chapter), as stated above and on the following page. This is followed by a short chapter (surah) from the Qur'an, such as "Mankind (Nas)" as stated on page 44.

STEP 9 (Continued)

أَلْحَمْدُ لِلَّهِ رَبِّ الْعَالَمِينَ .

Al-hamdu lillahi Rabbil-'alamin;
Praise be to Allah, the Lord of all the worlds;

أَلرَّحْمٰنِ الرَّجِيم .

Ar-Rahman nir-Raheem.
The Beneficent, The Most Merciful.[1]

مَالِكِ يَوْم الدِّين .

Maliki yaum mid-deen.
Master of the Day of Judgment.

إِيَّاكَ نَعْبُدُ وَ إِيَّاكَ نَسْتَعِينِ .

Iyyaka na'budu wa iyyaka nasta'een
You do we worship, and Your Aid we seek.[2]

إِهْدِنَا الصِّراطَ الْمُسْتَقِيم .

ihdenas seraa-tal mustaqeem,
Guide us on the straight way,[3]

صِراطَ الَّذِينَ أَنْعَمْتَ عَلَيْهِم .

Siraa-tal latheena, an'amta 'alay-him,
the way of those on whom You have bestowed Your Grace,

غَيْرِ الْمَغْضُوبِ عَلَيْهِم .

Ghay-ril maghdoobee 'alay-him,
Those whose [portion] is not wrath,

وَلا الضَّالِّينَ . آمِين.

Walad daaleen. Ameen.
and who go not astray. Amin.[1]

---

[1]Al-Fatiha (The Opening), continued from page 42.

STEP 9 (Continued)

بِسْمِ اللهِ الرَّخمنِ الرَّحيمِ

Bismillahir Ar-Rahman nir-Raheem.
In the Name of Allah,
The Beneficent, The Merciful.

قُلْ أَعوذُ بِرَبِّ النَّاسِ

Qul a'oothu be-Rabbin-nas
Say, I seek refuge with the Lord and Cherisher
of the people.

مَلِكِ النَّاسِ ، إلهِ النَّاسِ

Malikin-nas, Ilahin-nas
The King of the people, The God of the People.

مِنْ شَرِّ الْوَسْواسِ الْخَنَّاسِ

Min sharril was waasil khannas.
From the mischief of the whisperer [of evil],
who withdraws [after his whisper].

الَّذي يُوَسْوِسُ في صُدُورِ النَّاسِ

Allathee yuwas-wee-su fee sudurin nas.
[The same] who whispers into the hearts of the
people.

مِنَ الْجِنَّةِ وَ النَّاسِ

Minal jinnati wan-nas
among Jinns and among men.[1]

اللهُ أَكْبَرِ

Allahu Akbar.
Allah is the Greatest.

---

[1]Remain standing and recite Surah 114, Mankind (An-n as).

سُبْحـانَ رَبِّيَ الْـعَظيم

Subhana Rabbiyal 'atheem.

Highly glorified is my Lord, The Mighty.

سُبْحـانَ رَبِّيَ الْـعَظيم

Subhana Rabbiyal 'atheem.

Highly glorified is my Lord, The Mighty.

سُبْحـانَ رَبِّيَ الْـعَظيم

Subhana Rabbiyal 'atheem.

Highly glorified is my Lord, The Mighty.

Instructions: Assume the bending (ruku') position and recite the above.

STEP 11

سَمِعَ اللهُ لِمَنْ حَمِدهْ

Samee' Allahu liman hamidah.
Allah hears who praise Him.

رَبَّنـا وَلَكَ الْحَمْد

Rabbana wa lakal hamd.
Our Lord, and for You is the praise.

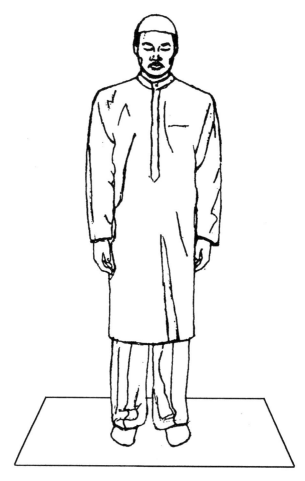

_____Instructions: While reciting the above, rise slowly from the bending (ruku')
position to the standing (qiyam) position, and while rising say, *Rabbana lakal
hamd.*

STEP 11 (Continued)

اللهُ أَكْبَر

Allahu Akbar.

Allah is the Greatest.

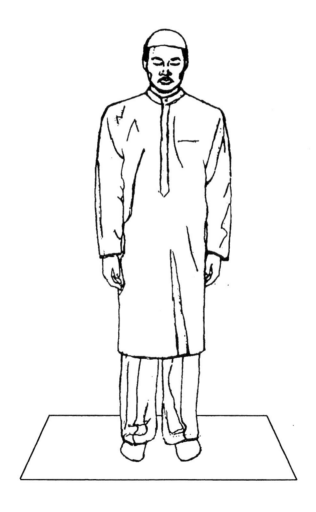

Instructions: After rising, say Takbir (Allahu-Akbar) as stated above.

STEP 12

سُبْحَانَ رَبِّيَ الأَغْلَى

Subhana Rabbiyal A'ala.

Highly glorified is my Lord, The Most High.

سُبْحَانَ رَبِّيَ الأَغْلَى

Subhana Rabbiyal A'ala.

Highly glorified is my Lord, The Most High.

سُبْحَانَ رَبِّيَ الأَغْلَى

Subhana Rabbiyal A'ala.

Highly glorified is my Lord, The Most High.

اللهُ أَكْبَر

Allahu Akbar.

Allah is the Greatest.

Instructions: Assume the prostrate (sajdah) position and recite Tasbih 3 times, and Takbir (Allahu-Akbar) once.

Note: This completes the second rak'ah.

اللهُمَّ اغْفِرْ لِي وَ ارْحَمْنِي

Allahum-maghfirlee war-hamnee.
O Allah, pardon me and have mercy on me.

اللهُ أَكْبَر

Allahu Akbar.
Allah is the Greatest.

Instructions: Rise from the prostrate (sajdah) position to the sitting (jalsah) position, and after rising, quickly say the above to yourself. After saying, "O Allah, pardon me and have mercy on me," say "Allahu Akbar," as you return to the prostrate (sajdah) position.

STEP 14

سُبْحَانَ رَبِّيَ الأَعْلَى

Subhana Rabbiyal A'ala.
Highly glorified is my Lord, The Most High.

سُبْحَانَ رَبِّيَ الأَعْلَى

Subhana Rabbiyal A'ala.
Highly glorified is my Lord, The Most High.

سُبْحَانَ رَبِّيَ الأَعْلَى

Subhana Rabbiyal A'ala.
Highly glorified is my Lord, The Most High.

اللهُ أُكْبَر

Allahu Akbar.
Allah is the Greatest.

Instructions: Return to the prostrate (sajdah) position and recite Tasbih 3 times, and Takbir (Allahu-Akbar) once, then rise to the sitting (jalsah) position.

التَّحِيَّاتُ لله

At-ta hi-yaatu lillahi,
All good, whether rendered by speech,

وَ الـصَّلَواتُ وَ الـطَّيِّبَاتُ

was-salawatu wat-tay-yibatu.
by prayer,by worship or by deeds, are all for Allah.

Instructions: after rising to the sitting (jalsah/qa'dah) position, recite "Tashahhud" as stated above and on the following page. To perform 3 or 4 rak'ahs, see instructions on page 52.

Note: When reciting "Tashahhud," the sitting position is referred to as qa'dah rahter than jalsah, even though both positions are physically the same. The only difference is in the recitation.

STEP 15 (Continued)

السَّلامُ عَلَيْكَ أَيُّها النَّبِيُّ

As-salaamu 'alayka ay-yuhan-nabiyyu
Peace be on you O Prophet

وَرَحْمَةُ اللهِ وَبَرَكاتُه

wa rahmatul laahee wa barakatuh.
and the Mercy and Blessings of Allah.

أَلسَّلامُ عَلَيْنَا

As-salaamu 'alayna
Peace be on us

وَعَلى عِبَادِ اللهِ الصَّالِحِين

wa 'ala'eebaadillah his-saaliheen.
and the righteous servants of Allah.

أَشْهَدُ أَنْ لا إِلَهَ إِلاَّ اللهُ

Ashhadu anla e-laaha ill Allahu.
I bear witness that there is no god except Allah.

وَأَشْهَدُ أَنَّ مُحَمَّدًا عَبْدُهُ وَرَسُولُه

*Wa ashhadu anna Muhammadan
'abduhu wa rasulluh.*
And I bear witness that Muhammad is His
Slave and Messenger.

Instructions: Remain in the sitting (qa'dah) position and recite the above.
Note: If the prayer consists of three rak'ahs, repeat STEPS 9 through 18.
If the prayer consists of four rak'ahs, repeat STEPS 1 through 18. In the third
and fourth rak'ahs of prayer, no verses from the Qur'an are recited after saying
"The Opening Chapter (Al-Fatiha)."

اللـهُمَّ صَلِّ عَلى مُحَمَّدٍ ، وَعَلى آلِ مُحَمَّد

Allahuma sal-lee 'ala Muhammad
wa'ala ali Muhammad
O Allah, praise and venerate Muhammad
and the family of Muhammad,

كَمَا صَلَّيْتَ عَلَى إِبْرَاهِيمَ ، وَعَلَى آلِ إِبْرَاهِيمَ

kama sallayta 'ala Ibraheema
wa 'ala alee Ibraheema.
as You praised and venerated Abraham
and the family of Abraham.

وَبَارِكْ عَلى مُحَمَّدٍ ، وَعَلى آلِ مُحَمَّدٍ

Allahumma baarik 'ala Muhammad
wa 'ala ali Muhammad,
O Allah, bless Muhammad and the
family of Muhammad,

كَمَا بَارَكْتَ عَلَى إِبْرَاهِيمَ ، وَعَلَى آلِ إِبْرَاهِيمَ

kama baarakta 'ala Ibraheema
wa 'ala alee Ibraheema.
as You blessed Abraham and the
family of Abraham.

فِي الْعَالَمِينَ

Fil-aalameena,
In the worlds,

إِنَّكَ حَمِيدٌ مَجِيد

Innaka Hameedum Majid.
surely You are Praised and Magnified.

Instructions: Remain sitting and recite al-sala 'ala-l-Naabiyy (prayer for the Prophet ﷺ) as stated above.

STEP 17

السَّلامُ عَلَيْكُمْ وَرَحْمَةُ الله

As-salaamu 'alaykum wa rahmatullah.

Peace be on you and the Mercy of Allah.

Instructions: Turning the face to the right (Right Salam), with the eyes looking down over the right shoulder, recite the above.

السَّلامُ عَلَيْكُمْ وَرَحْمَةُ الله

As-salaamu 'alaykum wa rahmatullah.
Peace be on you and the Mercy of Allah.

Instructions: To finish the prayer, turn the face to the left (Left Salam), with the eyes looking down over the left shoulder, and recite the above.
Note: This completes the prayer service of two rak'ahs.

Instructions: In the sitting (jalsah or qa'dah) position, the toes of the right foot touch the ground. The left foot is spread under the right side of the body with its left side in contact with the ground. The hands rest on the thighs with palms down and fingers extending to the ends of the knees. Should a person be unable to place the feet in the above position, they may be positioned under them in whatever way possible. See illustration, page 40, STEP 7 for front view. See next page for illustration and instructions for the woman's sitting position.

STEP 16 (Continued)

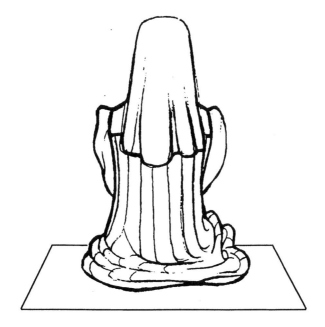

Instructions: The sitting (jalsah/qa'dah) rearview position for the woman is the same as for the man if one is physically able to do so.

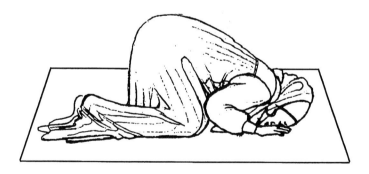

Instructions: The woman in the prostrate (sajdah) position is to put her elbows on her thighs, slighty off the floor, keeping them close to her abdomen and thighs.

Additional Supplications

اللـهمَّ إنَّكَ أنْتَ الـسَّلامُ وَمِنْكَ الـسَّلامُ

Allahuma antas salamu
wa minkas salamu.
O Allah, You are The Peace,
and from you comes peace.

تَبَـارَكْتَ وَتَعَـالَـيْتَ يـا ذا الـجَلالِ وَالإِكْرام

Tabarakta ya-thal jalaalee wata'alayta wal-ikram.
Blessed are you of Majesty and Bounty.■

Instructions: To offer additional supplications after prayer, you can remain in the sitting position. You may assume the position as above or one that is comfortable. The above supplication or those on the following page may be offered.

Additional Supplications (Continued)

رَبَّنَا آتِنَا فِي الدُّنْيَا حَسَنَةً

Rab-ban-na at-ti-na fid doon-ya has-an-na-tan,
Our Lord, give us what is good in this world,

وَفِي الْآخِرَةِ حَسَنَة

wa fil ak-he-rat-ti has-an-na-tan,
and also what is good in the Hereafter,

وَقِنَا عَذَابَ النَّارِ

wa kee-na athaa--ban-naar.
and save us from the torment of the Fire.■

— — — — — — — — — — — — — — — — — —

أَللَّهُمَّ أَعِنَّا عَلَى ذِكْرِكَ وَشُكْرِكَ

Allah-hum-ma a'in-na 'ala thik-ree-ka wa shu-kree-ka
O Allah! Help us so that we may remember You,

وَحُسْنِ عِبَادَتِك

wa hus-nee 'ibaa-da-tik
and adore You in the best way.■

— — — — — — — — — — — — — — — — — —

لَا إِلٰهَ إِلَّا اللهُ وَحْدَهُ لَا شَرِيكَ لَهُ

La-e-laa-ha ill lal-la-hu,
wah-da-hu la sha-reek-al-lah;
There is no god but Allah,
He is One and has no partner;

لَهُ الْمُلْكُ وَلَهُ الْحَمْدُ

La-who mul-ku wa la-hul ham-do,
Sovereignty and praise are for Him,

وَهُوَ عَلَى كُلِّ شَيْءٍ قَدِير

wa who-wa 'ala kul-lee shay-'in Qa-deer.
and He has full authority over everything.■

Glossary

A<u>dh</u>an: The call to prayer pronounced loudly to indicate that the time of prayer is due.

Al-Fatiha: "The Opening." The first Surah of the Qur'an.

'Asr: Afternoon prayer, time.

Din: A comprehensive "Way of life." Literally, anything adhered to, such as Din of Islam (Islamic ideology).

Fard: An obligatory action. If the individual performs the action, then he or she is rewarded. Whereas, the failure to perform the action results in a punishment.

Fajr: Dawn or early morning before sunrise.

Ghusl: Taking a complete bath in a religious, ceremonial way. This is necessary for one who is junub (one who is considered impure, having a legal, lawful sexual relation; a wet dream for both male and female or for the ending of the mentrual period of women).

Hadith: The traditions of Prophet Muhammad ﷺ, his sayings.

Iqamah: The statements of the Adhan, reduced so that they are repeated once in the Iqamah, except the last occurrence of Allahu Akbar. The prayer is offered immediately after the Iqamah.

'Isha': Evening prayer, the time for which starts about one-half hour after sunset.

Jalsah: The sitting position in the prayer, assumed with the palms of the hands resting above the knees on the thighs, with the fingers slightly parted and extending the them to the knees.

Ma<u>gh</u>rib: Sunset prayer.

Niyyah: Intention, purpose, vow.

Nas: Mankind, the 114th Surah of the Qur'an.

Qa'dah: The sitting position in prayer in which the Tashahhud is recited. The jalsah and qa'dah positions are the same with the exception that the words recited are different.

Qiyam: The posture of standing in prayer.

Rak'ah: Prayer positions, consists of standing, bowing and two prostrations.

Ruku: The position in prayer in which the head is bent forward, with the palms of the hands resting on the knees while the arms are stretched.

Sajdah: Prostration in Prayer. Touching the ground with the forehead, nose, both hands, knees and the tips of the toes. The title of the 32nd Surah of the Qur'an. A Surah by the recitation of which prostration becomes essential when certain verses are read.

Surah: A row or series. Strictly used for chapters of the Qur'an

Sunnah: Prophet Muhammad's ﷺ way of life. Consists of the sayings (hadith), actions and silent approvals of the Prophet ﷺ. All the traditions and practices of the Prophet ﷺ that have become as models to be followed by the Muslims.

Ta'awwuz: I seek refuge with Allah from Satan, the accursed (A'oothu billaahee minash shaytaanir-rajeem).

Takbiratul-Ihram: The first takbir of saying, "Allahu Akbar," in the beginning of a regular prayer and facing the Qiblah.

Tasbih: The expression, "Subhannah Allah," Pure and glorified are You, O Allah. Declaring that Allah is free of any imperfection and impurity.

Tashahhud: Testimony. I bear witness that there is no god except Allah. And I bear witness that Muhammad is His Servant and Messenger."

Tasmiyah: Bismillah (With the Name Allah).

Tayammum: Ablution (Wudu) performed with dust or sand when water is not easily obtainable. Put hands over the clean earth and then pass the palms of each in the back of the other hand, blow off the dust and then pass the hands over the face.

Thana': "Pure and glorified are You, O Allah. Blessed is Your Name, and exalted is Your Majesty, and there is nothing worthy of worship except You."

Wudu: Ablution made before saying the prayers in the traditional manner as described in hadith.

Witr: An odd number, optional, odd numbered Rak'ah prayers, performed after 'Isha' in which Du'a-al-Qunut is recited. Usually, three Rak'ahs are performed, but any odd number is acceptable. Properly called, Shaf'il Witr.

Zuhr: Noon, midday prayer.

Bibliography

Al-Bukhari, Abu Abdullah Muhammad b. Isma'il. *Sahih Bukhari*, Translation of the Meanings by Dr. Muhammad Muhsin Khan, Madinah, Saudi Arabia: Islamic University, Al-Madinah.

Ali, Abdullah Yusuf. *Holy Qur'an*, Text, Translation and Commentary, P. O. Box 6089, Beirut, Lebanon. Under supervision of Dar al-Arabia.

Maududi, Sayyid Abu A'la. *The Meaning of the Qur'an*, Arabic text with Translation and Commentary, Islamic Publications Ltd, 13-E, Shahalam Market, Lahore, Pakistan, Seventh Edition, 1985.

Muslim, Abu Husain. *Sahih Muslim*, compiled under the title, "Al-Jami'-Us-Sahih, translated by Abdul Hamid Siddiqi,Sh. Muhammad Ashraf, Lahore, Pakistan, 1975.

Siddiqi, Abdul Hamid. *Kitab Al-Salat*, Introduction to Sahih Muslim, Vol. I, p. 206, as translated into English, Sh. Muhammad Ashraf, Kashmiri Bazar, Lahore, Pakistan, January 1975.

S. Muhammad Tufail, *The Qur'an Reader*, An Elementary Course in Reading the Arabic Script of the Qur'an, The San Fernando Muslim Women's Association, The Mosque, Prince Albert Street, San Fernando, Trinidad West Indies, First Edition, April 1974.

Index

Now is the time to order copies of this historic first edition of Muslim Daily Prayers for yourself, your friends, and family members.

MUSLIM DAILY PRAYERS

A Learner's Guide
How to perform two, three and four rak'ahs
Arabic Pronunciation CD or Tape included

Introduction by
Minister Louis Farrakhan

Order Form

Please send me _____copies of the first edition of Muslim Daily Prayers, with introduction by Minister Louis Farrakhan, for which I enclose a cashier's check (or money order) in the amount of $_____
Cost for book with CD is $12.50. Add $3.25 for shipping and handling.

Please Print Clearly

Name_____

Address_____

City, State, Zip_____

Make all cashiers checks (or money orders) payable to:

Final Call
734 W. 79th Street
Chicago, IL 60620
www.finalcall.com